CORAL REEFS

Printed in China

02   03   04   05   06   5   4   3   2   1

Library of Congress Cataloging-in-Publication Data
Sheppard, Charles (Charles R.C.)
Coral Reefs: ecology, threats & conservation / Charles Sheppard.
p. cm. – (Worldlife Library)
Summary: Describes the nature, growth, location, and ecology of coral reefs.
Includes bibliographical references and index.
ISBN 0-89658-220-5 (pbk.: alk. paper)
1. Coral reef ecology – Juvenile literature. 2. Coral Reef conservation – Juvenile literature.
3. Coral reefs and islands – Juvenile literature. 4. Endangered ecosystems – Juvenile literature.
[1. Coral reefs and islands. 2. Coral reef ecology. 3. Ecology.] I. Title. II Series.
QH541.5.C7 S44 2002
577.7'89 – dc21

2002003005

Distributed in Canada by Raincoast Books, 9050 Shaughnessy Street, Vancouver, B.C. V6P 6E5
Published by Voyageur Press, Inc.
123 North Second Street, P.O. Box 338, Stillwater, MN 55082 U.S.A.
651-430-2210, fax 651-430-2211
books@voyageurpress.com   www.voyageurpress.com

Educators, fundraisers, premium and gift buyers, publicists, and marketing managers:
Looking for creative products and new sales ideas? Voyageur Press books are available at special discounts when purchased in quantities, and special editions can be created to your specifications. For details contact the marketing department at 800-888-9653.

Photographs copyright © 2002 by

Front cover © Gary Bell/Seapics.com
Back cover © Mark Conlin/Seapics.com
Page 1 © Colin Baxter
Page 3 © Jeff Sniadach
Page 4 © Colin Baxter
Page 6 © Jeff Jaskolski/Seapics.com
Page 8 © Kurt Amsler/Ardea London
Page 9 © David B. Fleetham/Seapics.com
Page 10 © Mark Webster/Oxford Scientific Films
Page 12 © Mark Conlin/Seapics.com
Page 13 © B. Jones & M. Shimlock/NHPA
Page 14 © Colin Baxter
Page 16 © Jeff Sniadach
Page 18 © Colin Baxter
Page 19 © Colin Baxter
Page 20 © Gary Bell/Seapics.com
Page 23 © Jean-Paul Ferrero/Ardea London
Page 24 © Colin Baxter
Page 27 © Colin Baxter
Page 28 © Jeff Sniadach
Page 30 © Michael Aw/Seapics.com
Page 31 © Pam Kemp/Oxford Scientific Films

Page 32 © Colin Baxter
Page 35 © Doug Perrine/Seapics.com
Page 36 © Bernhard Edmaier/Science Photo Library
Page 39 © Kurt Amsler/Ardea London
Page 41 © D. Parer & F. Parer-Cook/Ardea London
Page 42 © Doug Perrine/Seapics.com
Page 45 © B. Jones & M. Shimlock/NHPA
Page 46 © Doug Perrine/Seapics.com
Page 49 © David B. Fleetham/Seapics.com
Page 50 © Franco Banfi/Seapics.com
Page 51 © Marli Wakeling/Seapics.com
Page 53 © Robert Yin/Seapics.com
Page 54 © Colin Baxter
Page 56 © Howard Hall/Seapics.com
Page 57 © James D. Watt/Seapics.com
Page 58 © Colin Baxter
Page 61 © Kurt Amsler/Ardea London
Page 62 © Colin Baxter
Page 63 © Colin Baxter
Page 65 © Trevor McDonald/NHPA
Page 66 © Michael McCoy/Science Photo Library
Page 69 © Franco Banfi/Seapics.com

CORAL REEFS

Charles Sheppard

WORLDLIFE
LIBRARY

Voyageur Press

Contents

Some corals, like this Goniopora, in the Great Barrier Reef, grow to cover many square yards.

A Dive on a Coral Reef

With an air tank on my back, I float down to the reef through clear, tropical water off a coral island in a necklace of atolls running across the Indian Ocean. Away from the tropical sun and now bathed by cool blue water, my first impression is of thousands of fishes which create a confusing kaleidoscope of color and movement. Schools of fusiliers or silversides pass beside me in mid-water, harried by handfuls of swift predators like jacks or barracuda, which slice into the schools, trying to single out one or two individuals for food. Below them, colorful fish of all sizes and shapes hug the surface of the corals, flitting from coral to crevice, searching for food while trying not to become food themselves. Many shelter in branches of corals, backing away from me as I swim past, cautiously emerging again only after I have moved on. Colorful butterfly fish dart in pairs, and parrotfish swoop along in chaotic schools, scraping seaweed from the rock to eat; the riot of color and movement is overwhelming.

Then I focus on the corals themselves: in the shallows I can see the stubby branching forms, tough and resistant to waves, and note that these include many which are at least ten years old, healthy and vibrant, yellow and red. Some are dead, but there is nothing too unusual about that provided they remain a small minority. Moving slightly deeper I enter a zone of large table corals 7 feet (2 meters) across, sturdy despite their fragile appearance. All around these I observe countless kinds of coral boulders, with brain-like patterns or star patterns, and several huge corals whose size and identity tell me they are several hundred years old. Deeper still I can see a field of leafy, yellow coral scrolls in the darker water below me, but today I must stay in the shallows for a long time, so I do not go down to see them because of the greater water pressure there. Tomorrow, maybe. Most of the corals around me are stony, but some are soft and flexible, and amongst them all are tall sea fans, waving in the gentle currents. Each of the thousands of species in this riot of life has its own ecological role to play.

This is a research dive and my purpose is to monitor the health and diversity of the reef. The main task this morning is to work at 50 feet (15 meters) deep where, with the help of my buddy diver, I unroll a long tape measure and gently lay it across the reef to get some detailed measurements. I have to record the distance along the tape at which every coral starts and ends. This standard method of recording will continue until my buddy, who is dive leader today, tells me it is time to surface. I become lost in the task, and though I never lose sight of the beauty of the mauve, turquoise and red colors of the corals, I do not really notice any longer the multitude of fishes which so caught my gaze when I first entered. It is easy to get lost in the work, and only afterwards does my buddy diver tell me about the number of black-tip reef

Coral grouper in the Maldives, Indian Ocean.

sharks that cruised curiously by. I never know how much she is exaggerating…

Before the air in our tanks gets low my buddy diver signals that our time is up and we have to surface. Divers should not stay too long at any depth deeper than a few feet or they can run into decompression problems. We wind in the tape, and drift in a slow, controlled manner upward towards our waiting inflatable boat. We watch a school of eagle rays flap gracefully by, staying well offshore. Every day brings something memorable here. Sometimes we have seen giant manta rays, or a hammerhead shark passing by, a school of dolphins, and quite often some turtles. The variety is endless. Our boatman is expecting us, and knows we are surfacing from the changing pattern of our exhaled bubbles as they break the water's calm surface. He helps us pull our dive kit into the boat – it may be weightless underwater but all the hoses, air regulators, wet buoyancy aids and the tank itself are heavy above it. Then we pull ourselves over the sides and talk about the dive as we unclip the boat from its mooring. We wind our way through a passage in the shallows to a beach of coarse white sand near our base.

The beach itself is made from ground-up coral. This atoll is in a rainy part of the world, and behind the beach is a fringe of palm trees, planted long ago for their coconuts. This used to be a valuable crop, but the plantation is deserted now. We carry our kit to our campsite and meet up with others who are also returning from their morning research dives, stepping over hermit crabs on the shore, and passing very

Schooling racoon butterfly fish on a Hawaiian reef.

quietly by bushes filled with nesting and incredibly unafraid terns, boobies and frigate birds. A little further along the shore we can see fresh turtle tracks as well, a hawksbill turtle from its size, a species threatened because some people still want to make trinkets from its gorgeous, translucent shell. I feel that on this diving expedition my colleagues and I have glimpsed again a part of an ancient and timeless ecosystem, something that has been developing for many millennia. We all hope our work will help to ensure that this part of the coral reef world will continue to be as rich in the future as it is today.

What are Corals and Coral Reefs?

Corals are simple and primitive animals called polyps, like tiny sea anemones. They have a small fleshy body, with a ring of tentacles with stinging cells on top which catch tiny animals such as larvae for food. Where they differ from anemones is that they secrete limestone rock beneath their bodies, making little cups in which each one sits. This difference – the ability to make a supporting skeleton for themselves – is crucial, and is the reason for the existence of reefs. The polyps grow upwards almost all the time, expanding their skeleton as they go, and while they grow upward they also divide by budding off identical twins, which also continue to grow upwards and bud some more. They keep doing this year after year, and large colonies may be as much as 500 years old. These giants may contain millions of tiny, identically twinned polyps, each one sitting in its own tiny cup of limestone.

Each species grows and buds in different ways, resulting in different and characteristic shapes. Some grow branches, forming thickets of staghorn, bushes, or flat tables as long as a diver is tall. In these branching forms each polyp is usually just one tenth of an inch or less in width (1 to 2 millimeters). Kinds with much larger polyps may form domes with beautifully sculpted surfaces with stars, meandering valleys or clusters of flower-like projections. Many deeper corals grow into sheets, whorls or scrolls which project out from the reef into the water. Some have very sharp spines. Together, the hundreds of different species produce collections of architectural masterpieces, varying in color as well as shape.

Most of these tiny animals need light to grow. This is because their tissues contain millions of single-celled plant cells which, like plants everywhere, use light to make sugars in a process called photosynthesis. The sugars and oxygen made are used by the animal,

Close-up of a gorgonia, commonly known as a sea fan, at Ras Mohammed, northern Red Sea. The polyps have tentacles extended, to trap passing planktonic prey.

and likewise the products of the polyps, which are carbon dioxide and nutrients, are used by the captive plant cells. In this way an efficient symbiosis guarantees a useful arrangement for both parties. It is this need to gather light which determines some of the shapes that corals adopt. Other factors affecting their shapes are their resistance to waves – shallow forms are generally tough or sturdy, but species which grow deep enough to avoid the waves tend to be fragile and thin.

Together these corals grow into reefs. The skeletons of the largest corals are durable and form huge solid rocks, but even the fragile corals contribute to the reef-building process. Many become ground-up into sand when they die, which settles into cracks and crevices where, over many years, it resolidifies into durable forms of limestone. But much of the sand is pumped up onto beaches by the waves. All coral sand is white – the color of pure limestone – and this gives rise to the white beaches so typical of a coral sea. This sand can become consolidated into the island itself and so, in this way, corals maintain not only their own reefs but also help make many of the countless islands which lie scattered across the tropical seas.

Table coral with other stony and soft corals providing shelter for schools of fish, Fiji (above). Most reefs have a mix of stony and hard corals, but some are dominated by soft corals (right).

Reefs of the World

Roughly between the tropics of Cancer in the north and Capricorn in the south, the sea is warm enough for corals to grow. The reefs that they create are the most elaborate and biologically rich structures that the world has ever seen. The province of coral reefs is not uniformly wide, but expands where currents of warm water push outwards from the equator, such as towards Japan from the warm pool of water in Southeast Asia, and constricts where cool polar currents cut into it, such as along the western coasts of the Americas. Reef corals need light, so they grow only where the water is suitably shallow. Corals are not very tolerant of freshwater, as a result they do not grow where rivers flow into the sea. Nor can they withstand high-levels of sediment or nutrients, so they are missing from great swathes of ocean which have muddy, shallow sea floors. They are, in short, very particular about where they live, but that still leaves a great deal of suitable ocean where they flourish very well.

There are two major reef provinces, divided by the great land barriers of the Americas and Africa. The Atlantic province contains the Caribbean and surrounding areas, the coasts of North and South America, north to Bermuda and south along Brazil, and a few spots across on the West African side. The other, much larger, province is the Indo-Pacific, which extends from East Africa and Arabia, including the Red Sea, through the Indian Ocean to the rich island groups of Southeast Asia and the Great Barrier Reef of Australia, then on through the islands of the Pacific. Further east than Hawaii and Polynesia, the huge expanses of deep ocean have few areas with water shallow enough for coral, apart from a few island groups such as the Galapagos. The western seaboard of the Americas is mostly unsuitable,

Shallow finger corals in Hawaii. Several different species form tough, stubby colonies in shallow water throughout the Indo-Pacific ocean, where wave energy can be strong.

so reefs are sparse there. From the point of view of marine life, the Indian and Pacific oceans are really one – the Indo-Pacific ocean. Land forms no barrier between these oceans; quite the reverse in fact, as the thousands of small islands of Southeast Asia provide a lot of ideal coral habitat. Indeed, the number of corals in Southeast Asia is higher than anywhere else in the world. This coral province used to be even bigger. Before the continents drifted to

their present positions, there was one continuous belt of warm water, called the Tethys Sea, stretching all around the world, incorporating all the present tropical oceans and the Mediterranean Sea too. When Central America emerged above the sea to form a land barrier in the Miocene and Pliocene about four to seven million years ago, the Atlantic province became separated, and after its isolation it evolved its own group of corals.

Kinds of Reefs

Corals form several kinds of reef in this tropical belt. Some rest on different geological foundations, some sit on substrates that are much older than others, while some lie on continental shelves or on subsiding islands. But all are formed with the common, underlying theme of coral growth. Corals and other reef species, especially some forms of stony algae, create vast quantities of durable limestone rock as they grow. In effect, corals build their own substrate – the reef.

The simplest coral reefs fringe a rocky shore. The layer of rock that builds up may be quite thin. These simple reefs, like almost all others, have a horizontal expanse at the level of the low tide – a reef flat – which stretches seaward for tens or even hundreds of feet. This reef flat supports some corals, but the shallow water here can become very hot and is generally too hostile an environment for very much marine life. At the edge of the reef flat, however, the surface dips, usually quite sharply, and descends to great depths. Most reef life is always found on these slopes, and it is here where the diving is the best, and where the color, variety and abundance of life is greatest. The reef slope is the growing edge of the reef, with the clearest water, and it is where most reef species want to be.

Corals are animals, but they contain millions of algal cells within their tissues. The animal and plant components live in a symbiotic harmony, which is mutually beneficial. The wastes from one are nutrients for the other and so a tight and efficient recycling takes place between them to the benefit of both. Plants need light, so the whole assemblage cannot live where it is too dark, and this limits the deepest extent of reef corals, and of active reef growth, to about 200 feet (60 meters) deep. At their shallowest extreme, corals cannot live out of the water above low tide level. These two considerations control the shape of the reef. Put simply, they grow upwards in shallow, sunlit water to the height of the low tide, and the edges of the reef grow outwards, away from the shore, until there is no more foundation for the corals to grow on. As the reef grows outwards, its slope may steepen, becoming vertical in places, and when a growing edge extends out too far, it may overhang and even slump. All the while, corals live and die. They are ground down into rubble and sand, and these particles, totaling thousands of tons for each mile of reef, also become important components of a coral reef. Thus the basic reef profile of a horizontal reef flat at low tide level, followed by a plunging reef slope, is maintained everywhere in the world.

The land on which reefs grow varies enormously too, adding much fine detail to this basic pattern. This land may be a stable continental shelf, an old subsiding volcano, or a platform being pushed up by immense tectonic forces. Where a reef is broad, it may have become eroded behind its growing edge, making a navigable channel parallel to land. There may be a shallow ridge running along the outer edge of the shelf, with islands or sand cays. In this case the reef may develop into a barrier reef, perhaps far offshore. Added to these, remnants of ancient reefs may themselves provide good foundations for new reef growth, so long-dead reefs may help determine the shapes of new, living ones. We know that sea level about 15,000 years ago was about 500 feet (150 meters) below its present level, when vast amounts of water became locked up as ice during the long ice ages. Then, when the ice started melting, the sea level rose over just a few thousand years to the present level which it reached about 8000 years ago. The different amounts of rainfall over these

long periods, different erosion patterns and different rates of coral growth, have all increased the range of shapes of fringing and barrier coral reefs.

Then there are atolls, irregular rings of reefs usually with small islands, located in mid-ocean far from land. These rise steeply from oceanic depths of several miles to protrude today just above the level of low tide, and their islands are perhaps only 3 to 6 feet (1 to 2 meters) high. Encircled by the atoll rim is a shallow lagoon only a few tens of feet deep which, viewed from the air, appears pale blue or turquoise in contrast with the deep oceanic blue outside the atoll. Atolls have passes into their lagoons cut through their rims whose depths are commonly the same as the depth of the lagoon itself, which are kept open by scouring streams of sediment. Some of the reef's most dramatic forms of marine life can be seen here. Atolls and their islands are the tips of columns of limestone which may be several miles high, the columns in turn resting on volcanic rock. These old volcanic mountains initially provided the foundation for the coral

The fringing reef around Lizard Island, an island on the Great Barrier Reef (above). Here, the diversity of corals is extremely high. Staghorn corals in a sheltered lagoon, Great Barrier Reef (left). Corals in sheltered areas may grow long, slender branches, because the wave energy in such lagoonal areas is generally weak and insufficient to break the branches.

Underwater seascape, Fiji, south Pacific. Outcrops create habitats for numerous schools of small fishes, in this case Anthias. The deeper red kind is a male, and the gold colored fishes are his harem of females. If the male dies, the dominant female will become a male and take his place in the school.

reef growth, but have subsided gradually for millions of years, during which time the upward growth of corals around their shores matched the rate of subsidence. The present shape of the atoll near sea level is, in part, inherited from millennia of growth.

The variety of fringing reefs, barriers and atolls is considerable, and the boundaries of each type blend smoothly into each other. Limestone is a soft, basic rock and rain is slightly acidic. Therefore, every time in geological history when a reef has been raised above sea level, either from a fallen sea level during an ice age, or from tectonic uplifting, rain has dissolved part of the rock and added even more variety of shape. The acid rain etches holes into the limestone reefs, carving long tunnels and huge caverns deep into its fabric. The so-called 'blue holes' in reefs are formed this way, many famous ones being found in the Caribbean. These are sudden and unexpectedly deep shafts sunk into a shallow reef, and their blue color comes from the color change of their deep water. These features all add greater variety and habitat.

The Making of a Reef

The way in which corals actually build a reef is a complicated story, and one equally important as how the corals themselves come into being. Sometimes corals merely grow on top of older, dead corals – it can be as simple as that – and some small fringing reefs are formed in this way. Mostly though, several other factors come into play. Corals are broken down immediately after they die by waves and by a range of boring and tunneling organisms which grind up the reef's rocky skeletons into rubble, fine sand and silt. This sediment then packs itself into crevices, where it stabilizes and gradually re-cements itself together into a reef fabric which is stronger than the original coral skeleton. If you drilled a core through most reefs you would see that the core's structure is a mixture of both this bonded matrix and of whole coral skeletons, the latter embedded in the former. You do not need to take a core if you know where to find a fossil reef which has been eroded by the weather, because in these you can see fossil corals entombed in their stony matrix, the corals often in their original, upright position of growth. Excellent examples occur in many parts of the world, and are best seen by divers, perhaps, along the Red Sea's diving centers, on many Caribbean islands, and in many parts of Southeast Asia.

One of the most important things about corals, therefore, is that they produce sand when they are dead. This, and the usually unsung factors that bond this sand together again such as chemical solution, microbial activity and others, is as important to reef building as the initial coral growth. This means that any reef organism which secretes limestone is important too. On some reefs, calcareous algae make as much sand as the corals do. These are seaweeds which, like corals, deposit large amounts of limestone within their tissues. Some, like the green seaweed *Halimeda*, are leafy, yet they secrete limestone in every one of their thousands of disk-like blades. This kind can dominate sand production; the Bahamas Banks, off the southeast coast of Florida, are full of it, for example. Others do not even look like plants and have the appearance of stones. These are 99 percent limestone with just a film of living plant material over their skeletal stone. Many reefs have at their seaward edge a belt of these stony red algae, growing in tough ridges which take the full force of the waves. It seems that these curious plants need severely turbulent water to survive, and their rocky strength has been estimated to be even greater than concrete. Many forms of life, not only corals, are crucial to the formation of coral reefs.

The results of these processes are rocky limestone structures which are famous for the diversity and profuseness of their life. They are the place where biologists want to go to understand ecological questions, where pharmacists want to go to examine the chemical makeup of many of their species. They are where fishermen want to go to benefit from their amazing productivity, and they are the place where divers want to go because they are, quite simply, the most spectacular places in the sea.

A maze of coral reefs and passages separated by sandy gullies, Hardy Reef, Queensland, Australia.

The Corals' Way of Life

Corals are the key to any coral reef. Each coral is a colony of small animals, called polyps, each individual looking a bit like a tiny sea anemone – a small sack of tissue with a mouth at the top surrounded by a ring of tentacles. Many species have polyps about half an inch (1 centimeter) in diameter, though many are much smaller at 0.04 inches (1 millimeter), and others have polyps which are several inches wide. It is their manner of growth that makes them so important. Every now and again they bud into two, by literally cleaving their bodies in half or by sprouting a daughter polyp off the side of the parent. The two resulting polyps remain attached to each other to varying degrees, and then each buds again, so that from one initial polyp there are four made, then eight, then 16, and so on. Each polyp is an individual to some extent, but remains connected to the others. Large colonies, hundreds of years old, contain millions of polyps which are all genetically identical.

The important point about this is that all the time the coral's undersurfaces are laying down a supporting, limestone skeleton. Limestone is almost entirely calcium carbonate, a mineral that the polyps extract from the seawater they grow in. So, to grow, a colony buds a little, the polyps deposit a little skeleton beneath themselves, they bud a little more, and so on, growing upwards and outwards, year after year. Dome-shaped colonies many feet in diameter may be 500 years old or more – the record from Asia apparently is over 700 years old – expanding their radius by up to half an inch (1 centimeter) each year. Branching forms grow faster, laying down less limestone in total, but extending their branches 4 inches (10 centimeters) each year. In all cases, the rock is a form of limestone called aragonite. Its growth rate depends in part on the water temperature, so a core through a large dome

Shallow soft corals and stony corals in a sheltered location of the Great Barrier Reef. The waves above them determine that they grow no higher than the average low tide level.

coral will show growth rings, like tree rings, which can be counted to determine the approximate age of the coral.

On the surface of a coral – say a typical boulder-shaped colony – may be numerous dish-shaped cups. Each is the location of a single polyp. In daytime the polyp is usually tightly retracted, so their rings of tentacles are not visible, but at night, each cup will be ringed with expanded tentacles. At the center of each cup the small mouth is usually visible as a dot of a different color. Brain corals are patterned with a series of valleys rather than cups. Polyps of these species separate less during budding, so that each valley contains a chain of connected polyps. Along the floor of the valley a row of mouths can be seen, and an elongated ring of tentacles surrounds them all.

The tissues of many reef building species are vibrantly colorful, though the dominant color is brownish-green, which comes from a layer of symbiotic algal cells contained in the tissues of the polyps themselves. The nature of the symbiosis means that both the algae and the animal polyp benefit from this liaison. Feeding by a coral is a mixture of using the products of the algae, whose photosynthesis produces carbohydrates which the coral needs, but they also capture tiny, planktonic animal prey, which the polyps trap using batteries of stinging cells in their tentacles. Over three-quarters of the energy needs from carbohydrates may be obtained from the captive plant cells, while the captured plankton provide essential nutrients and proteins.

A colony's shape and size is determined by what species it is, though each species can show variation depending on its immediate environment. In shallow water, corals must have tough skeletons – fragile forms cannot survive the pounding waves. Shallow species must also be tolerant to intense light, and any which grow in ponded basins on reef flats must also withstand temperatures which can reach that of a hot bath. On the other hand, species that live very deep in dimly lit parts of the reef slope, develop leafy shapes to trap as much light as possible. Their leaves are thin and fragile, but since they grow far deeper than the

Typical 'brain corals' amongst branching corals and pillars of stony corals in the Great Barrier Reef. Each species has characteristic colony shapes and surface patterns.

The middle depths of a reef slope off New Guinea. At mid-depths of 15 to 80 feet deep (5 to 25 meters) light is abundant, wave energy is not usually destructive, and diversity is greatest on a coral reef. Vase shaped soft corals reach towards the light, while the stony corals form plate-like skeletons or sheets that require less construction but which still hold out their surfaces to intercept the light. Almost all the living surfaces of corals are sloped at 45 degrees, which means that they will easily shed any sediment which falls upon them. Very little reef surface at these depths is left unoccupied — something, whether corals, soft corals or sponges will quickly settle on any spare substrate.

Competition for habitat is strong here, so diversity in crevices, overhangs and out on the surface is very high. Commonly overlooked on reefs is the large quantity of encrusting red algae and red and orange sponge, both of which may form small sheets on the rock or on dead parts of coral skeletons.

base of the destructive waves, their fragility does not matter so much, and what is important is that they can catch sunlight. But there is a problem with this, which is that a horizontal shape which catches most sunlight would also be smothered by a gentle rain of sediment, so they compromise by growing at an angle of about 45 degrees to let sediment slide off gently.

The most desirable places to live are the middle depths: not too shallow where waves would smash their skeletons, but not too deep or sheltered where sediment builds up; not so deep and dark that their plant cells cannot work efficiently, but not so bright they suffer damage. The most desirable locations are the mid-depths on reef slopes, between 16 to 80 feet (5 to 25 meters) deep, where there is a gentle current. This is the zone where coral diversity is greatest.

This means, however, it is also the place where there is the greatest competition for living space on the reef. Corals have to vie for space between both themselves and against other forms of life. Some corals survive and perpetuate themselves by rapid and copious reproduction. Others grow fast, to occupy space or to overgrow rivals quickly, like table corals that overtop and shade smaller species. Or they can use some defensive strategies in which they actively kill opponents which encroach into their space. Many can develop 'sweeper tentacles' around their colony perimeter, which are 20 times longer than normal tentacles and heavily loaded with stinging cells. When the time is right, after perhaps two weeks of developing them, following detection of a threat, they throw these tentacles onto their target one night and kill it. Another method many corals use if the range is smaller is to open up their body wall and throw a mass of digestive filaments over their opponent, literally digesting it away in a couple of hours. This, too, happens at night. Corals have to some degree a hierarchy, in which some species always beat others.

We might wonder why a dominant species does not monopolize the reef completely? In some limited areas they do, but generally there is a balance or an arms race in miniature.

Corals that dominate in one way may not reproduce as rapidly, or may not grow as fast as others. As in any ecosystem, there is an equilibrium. Assuredly, species which fail to measure up in any way at all will become extinct. We must remember that the fossil record tells us that for every species alive today, about 100 others have appeared, lived a while, and become extinct when they failed to compete sufficiently on the dynamic and changing reef. The result is that today there is a profusion of different species jostling for space to

live on any reef, each with their own tricks for survival, and commonly the reef's surface may be occupied by dozens or even hundreds of different species of corals and their relatives.

Soft Corals and Other Relatives

Corals have several important relatives. Soft corals are very similar, but instead of laying down a stony skeleton, they establish a rubbery matrix of organic matter. The skeletons of several kinds may be laced with strengthening stony spicules, but when these colonies of animals die, their organic skeletons disintegrate and disperse, leaving no trace. Soft corals can be very colorful, and polyps of many species contain symbiotic algae like their stony relatives. They show different strategies for survival — some species produce toxic chemicals which they diffuse into the water surrounding them, and others breed by extending runners out sideways to colonize space on the reef some distance away. In the Caribbean region, 'soft corals' are in the sea fan group of colonial animals. These are generally conspicuous because they can extend

Scene typical of a shallow reef, John Pennekant Coral Reef State Park, Florida. Sea fans and hardy corals frequent such areas. These sea fans are elevated up above the general surface of the reef.

their flexible branches more than 3 feet (I meter) above the reef surface, their tree-like structures giving their polyps some elevation into water where they can capture planktonic prey effectively.

Sea fans occur in the Indo-Pacific as well, but generally are less common than in the Caribbean, though where they do grow their size makes them very conspicuous. They more commonly occur in dark places, deeper on the reef, and on the walls of caves, where there is not enough light for corals. The fans themselves are composed of a tough but flexible skeleton, covered with and made by the huge numbers of tiny polyps that it supports, all extending tiny tentacles into the water. Several species of sea fans orient themselves across a prevailing current, even if the flow is very gentle, as this allows each polyp greatest exposure to the water and the best chance of capturing some of the drifting particles of food.

Other more distant relatives include the precious black coral, not a true coral at all, but similar in general body plan. In this case though, its harder, organic skeleton can be polished into a black, glossy shine, so this group of species is collected to cut and turn into jewelry. Then there are the fire corals. Their skeletons are stony, like the true corals, but their stinging cells are particularly powerful, as any diver brushing a patch of exposed skin across one will remember. In this case it is not only that the stinging cells inject a particularly poisonous toxin, more that the hair-like stings of this group are strong enough to penetrate human skin, so that we notice them. It is the stings of these colonial animals, called nematocysts, which help to characterize the whole group. Borne in clusters in the tentacles, especially at the tips, the batteries of stinging cells include tiny triggers that are sensitive to touch, causing the stingers to fire. There are several kinds: some inject a toxin, paralyzing the prey extremely quickly; while others have barbs which simply hang onto the prey that has been caught. A coral cannot move, so a successfully poisoned zooplankton which then floats away is no use to the polyp which caught it. The toxin is very fast acting, as you can see if you hold a torch to a coral during a dive at night. The light attracts plankton, some of which are large enough to see with the naked eye. If you hold the torch right at the tentacles, some plankton will soon brush against them and immediately be caught, to struggle for only a second. Then the tentacle pulls the captured prey in, and stuffs it into its mouth.

Efficient though they are at capturing prey, most of the corals and soft corals found on reefs, and even their relatives such as sea anemones, contain symbiotic algae. The products of the plants' photosynthesis give the coral much of its energy, more than is obtained by capturing prey in many cases. This symbiosis is clearly a very successful mode of living. The seabed of a reef is, in one sense, a carpet of captive algae, and this is where the main source is of plants on a reef. They are invisible to the naked eye, but are plants nevertheless, providing the ecological foundation to much of the rest of the life on a reef. The energy gained by corals from having captive algal cells is substantial, allowing this group of colonial animals to have developed some of the ocean's biggest structures, and while there are some without algae, those usually live deep on the reef. To a considerable degree, the host corals regulate the numbers of algal cells in each polyp, and in a sense the algae are actively farmed. They inhabit one of the tissue layers of the polyp animals as well as a layer of the tissues which connect adjacent polyps together. Not only do they provide most of the carbohydrate energy for the polyps, they also greatly facilitate the process by which the coral lays down its limestone skeleton.

It is this fusion of polyps with their tiny captive algae which has allowed reef life to become so rich and diverse; the widespread symbiotic relationship has become one of the fundamental ecological characteristics of the coral reef community. It is certainly one of the features of the reef which allows it to work so efficiently and successfully. Other important characteristics are looked at later, but this successful fusing of animal and plant, which has underpinned the success of the reef system for so long, may go very wrong if corals suffer too much stress. When it does go wrong, the whole reef comes under threat, as we see later.

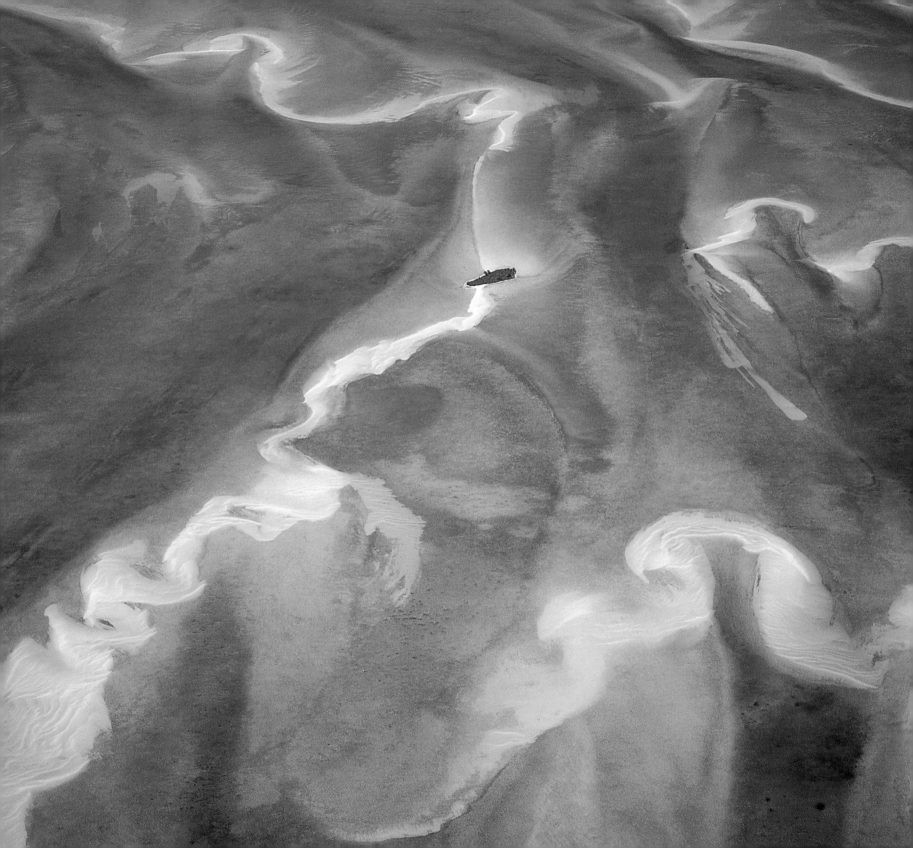

Special Reef Areas

Reefs across the world can be grouped into many different categories: by country, by reef type or by diversity. All reef scientists and divers probably have their favorite areas, so a selection of five of the 'best' regions is very subjective. Five outstanding areas are briefly described here, which represent many of the world's reefs, and which are among my own favorite locations for both recreational diving and scientific research.

The Bahamas Bank

The Bahamas Bank, in the greater Caribbean region, is a vast shallow limestone bank, containing everybody's ideal of a group of coral islands. The islands are low lying, many with fossil reefs extending many feet above sea level. Some islands lie beside deep water, like the 'Tongue of the Ocean', a famous cut into the Bank, with huge underwater walls and spectacular diving. Reefs descend steeply to hundreds of feet, though reef life disappears well before that as light becomes too dim. You can swim among countless patches of shallow corals, commonly called 'coral gardens', and through spectacular fissures in the vertical walls. Between the coral reefs are vast plains of seagrass, or of calcareous green plants called *Halimeda*, which create as much sand as the corals. These banks support large local fisheries including that of the conch mollusk, a giant heavyweight of a shell, which is collected in huge numbers for its flesh. 'Blue holes' occur here too – caves and tunnels cut deep into the soft limestone by rains in past aeons when the whole bank was high and dry during a period of much lower sea level and high rainfall. These freshwater drainage channels now flooded by the sea make for some spectacular diving and exploration.

Part of the Bahamas Bank from the air. Massive sand banks made from ground-down coral and fragments of stony algae dominate these banks. Spectacular reefs are found in deeper water.

The Red Sea

Then there is the Red Sea, which is really a young ocean, a long narrow landlocked sea separating Africa from the Arabian peninsula. Born 30 to 40 million years ago, it is widening a few inches every year as Arabia moves north and rotates anti-clockwise. The forces that tear the continents apart are thought to be slowly flowing molten material deep within the earth. As the molten material flows by convection, huge plates of the Earth's crust are pushed along it and, when a tear rips a continent into two, then an ocean can be formed. The Atlantic formed in a similar way, but much earlier, so is a lot wider now. In the northern Red Sea are many diving centers, all benefiting from sheer coral walls and extremely clear water. Its huge depths close to shore, and its warm waters, are ideal for reef life which extends down the coasts of both Africa and Arabia. In the north especially, fringing reefs hug the shoreline, then further out to sea there are barriers of coral reefs stretching for a few hundred miles. Along both sides of the Red Sea there is a series of raised fossil reefs, all previously grown in shallow water but jolted tectonically upwards as the Red Sea has widened. Those nearest the sea are only about 6 to 13 feet (2 to 4 meters) high now, but older ones a few hundred feet inland form higher steps, and on the sides of all of them fossil corals can be seen. The Red Sea is especially rich in marine life. It has some of the clearest water because of the sea's low nutrient levels and because of the proximity to great depths. Although it is famous for its good diving sites, the area of rich reefs is actually limited mainly to the northern two-thirds.

Indian Ocean Atolls

Indian Ocean atolls occur in two main groups. One lies to the west – those of the Seychelles and others running south to Mauritius – and the other is a large, almost continuous chain running south from India, including: the Lakshadweep islands which are part of India; the Maldives, an independent Republic; and the Chagos archipelago, which is a British Territory.

These atolls are classic rings of reefs and islands, enclosing relatively shallow lagoons, each separated from each other by water sometimes several miles deep. Atoll islands have maximum elevations of no more than about 6 to 10 feet (2 or 3 meters), which is causing concern as sea levels rise. A few, most famously Aldabra atoll, are elevated higher, in some cases by changes in relative sea level since the time when they formed long ago, in other cases by upward jolts as continents move across the face of the Earth. As the volcanic mountains

on which these columns of limestone rest subside ever deeper beneath the surface, earthquakes cause jolts, both upwards and downwards, even fracturing some atolls. But given good coral growth, reefs have been able to grow upwards as their foundations subside, and they have kept pace with the rise in sea level. Atolls in the central oceans have some of the clearest water of all, so underwater you feel

immune to gravity. Steep cliffs, colorful coral gardens, caves and fissures are all present.

Pacific Volcanic Islands

If atolls are the classic low islands, Pacific volcanic islands are the typical 'high islands'. Volcanoes, many still active, rise above the sea floor, and now are ringed with reefs. Some reefs are fringes closely hugging the sides of the tall, green-clothed mountains, others are separated from their islands by channels of navigable water. The reefs circling almost all high islands are cut in some places by channels where reef has not grown, perhaps because the mouth of a small river drains freshwater from the mountains there. High islands ringed with reefs are strung across all tropical oceans but are more frequently associated perhaps with the western Pacific and many have island cultures which are centuries old, but with increased populations who place ever-greater demands on the reef resources, their sustainable way of life is disappearing. Their landscapes vary, from rainy, wet and very attractive, to fairly arid, scorched and dry, though in both cases the underwater scenery attracts divers from all over the world.

Great Barrier Reef

The Great Barrier Reef is the largest reef structure in the world, running down the east coast of Australia from the Torres Strait to south of the Tropic of Capricorn. I have spent many hours underwater on some of the varied structures, from some fairly murky reefs near shore to wonderful outer reefs on the edge of Australia's continental shelf and, in such places, I have seen a myriad of corals and fish. The Great Barrier Reef is not one single structure but consists of thousands of reefs, large barriers in the north and south, and hundreds of patch reefs in the central region. Most lie offshore leaving a channel many miles wide between the reef and continent. This wide channel is generally muddy, supporting seagrasses and mangroves along the shore itself, with only relatively few coral patches. Not surprisingly, given its size, the Great Barrier Reef has many different ecological zones. Some of these are arranged north-south, with a greater diversity of corals in the north, nearer the Equator. Other patterns occur across the reef, in this case determined by gradients of sedimentation (greater nearer the mainland) or of wave energy (greater nearer the outer edge). Its enormous variety of life is well protected and managed so we can hope that it will be conserved indefinitely for all to enjoy.

Capricorn Bunker group and Heron Island, Great Barrier Reef, from the air.

The Web of Life

On and above the reef is the richest assemblage of species found in the sea. In one small chapter we could only look at a tiny fraction of it, so, rather than try to describe some favorite examples, let us examine instead some key aspects of how it all works – of reef ecology. These include some of the essential principles which hold it all together in an integrated, living ecosystem.

We have already noted the crucial and central symbiosis between corals and their captive plants. This has allowed corals to develop into many shapes and sizes, and the three-dimensional structure of the reef surface that they make as a result is very important. It helps explain why the diversity of other forms of life is so high. Numerous branches and columns, the death and partial erosion of their skeletons, and the soft nature of the rock that permits many species to tunnel into it directly, all add a great deal of three-dimensional shapes and structures, providing a varied habitat with countless burrows, nooks and crevices for species to live in. Many predators use this three-dimensional relief to wait in ambush; many more species use it for shelter. Most of the fishes on a reef are carnivorous, waiting to capture prey from its surface, and because of this swarm of hungry predators hanging above them, most species which live on the surface of the reef are, not surprisingly, fairly cryptic in their habits. Living in or not very far from holes and gullies, they are quick to try and escape the attentions of the hordes of carnivores. Branching corals are the best places to observe this, because most are home to small schools of tiny and brightly colored fish which hover outside the branches to feed when they can, withdrawing into safety as soon as a large fish, or a diver, approaches. The three-dimensional structure is one important reason for the reef's diversity and, when it is destroyed, as is happening on many of the world's reefs, it is the loss of this structure as much as anything which causes the loss of biological richness.

Scraping Space to Live

The continuous production of sand has already been described as being crucial to coral reef growth. In fact, countless small, eroding and tunneling species that we hardly ever notice make a lot of the sand. Many species spend their whole lives out of sight, an understandable trait in an environment with so many hungry predators. But much of the sand is also made by several important groups of herbivores which create huge quantities of it when they scrape their seaweed food off the coral rock. Parrotfish especially are masters at this, excreting many tons of sand per hectare annually as they ingest a bit of surface rock each time they scrape it for their desired plant food. In doing so they produce fine sand, ideal for later cementation into durable rock. Their rasping also creates bare areas of rock, in bite-size patches, all over the reef. These bare areas are necessary for new coral larvae to settle on. Corals reproduce by means of larvae, which themselves are highly sought after as food, not only by fishes but also by other corals waiting with their millions of stinging tentacles. If one settles on a coral, or even next to one, its short life will soon be over. To survive, it needs a patch of rock a safe distance away from other corals, and provision of such patches is just what happens as a result of the parrotfishes' feeding.

On many reefs, sea urchins are important scrapers too, and the disturbance of the substrate that happens as they scrape their slow paths along the reef has similarly important ecological consequences. The newly scraped patches of bare space on the reef, a result of grazing by herbivorous groups of animals, both keeps down the fast-growing seaweeds, which otherwise would dominate the reef, and provides a great deal of safe, tentacle-free rock for the next generation of corals. The creation and recolonization, or turnover, of bare space on a reef is remarkably fast, given the slow growth and seemingly static nature of corals. The amount of bare space at any one time may be no more than a few percent of the whole reef

Mid-depths off Komodo Island, Indonesia, with numerous feather stars out feeding.

surface, but the exact nature of what life occupies any one point can change quite rapidly. One moment the point might be occupied by a coral, the next, when the coral dies, it may be algae. A time-lapse sequence of a reef would show not the static, still-life picture that we see on a single dive, but a dynamic and changing pattern. It is simply that we see things on a different timescale to the rate of activity and changing space ownership on a patch of reef, but once we understand that the reef does indeed have an active and continuously changing nature, we can understand much more about its ecology.

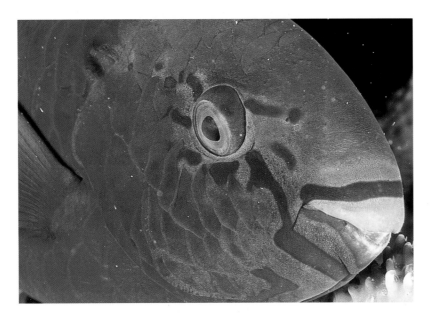

Damaging a Component

There are many aspects which could illustrate the dynamic nature of a reef, but the plant-herbivore one is crucial. Now we understand that a reef has a lively quality we can explore what might happen if we were to inadvertently knock out one ecological component of it, perhaps by overfishing one or two of its species. If the reef had been a static system, it perhaps might not matter too much to the overall ecological structure when a species disappears from it. But once we understand that there is a cohesive relationship between its many components we can see that if we remove one, the effect can be like removing a spring in a complicated network of springs; the whole system will shift to accommodate the change in tensions, and similarly on a reef, the system will adjust itself to the loss of a species. The adjustment may not be particularly noticeable, depending on the species removed, but it might just as easily, and often unexpectedly, result in a major ecological shift. Good examples of this are the consequences of the removal of grazing animals, or of disease, a common event these days.

Two Caribbean examples explain this concept well. In the 1980s disease wiped out the grazing sea urchin, *Diadema*, a black species with long, sharp spines. This was not only one of the very important grazers, keeping down the seaweeds that grow so easily and quickly in the Caribbean, but their continual scraping away of algae exposed the limestone beneath, making it available for organisms like corals to settle on. When the urchins died out, algae quickly dominated the reefs. Today, many Caribbean reefs are covered with weed as a result, to such an extent that many have few corals left. The other example is the removal of herbivorous fish, due to overfishing, which had a similar effect. To some degree the increased grazing by the other species could perhaps have compensated for the removal of one herbivore. But the problem in the Caribbean was that both major herbivore groups were removed together in several areas – the urchins by disease and the herbivorous fishes by overfishing. The result was a marked shift in the community, leading to heavy dominance by algae over huge expanses of reefs, to such a degree that it looks as though it will be very difficult, if not impossible, for corals ever to recover. As a consequence, huge areas of the reef system have settled into an alternative state, which seems perfectly stable. But one thing we must never do is to write-off a system. Certainly it seems unlikely that fishing will stop sufficiently for huge numbers of herbivorous fish to return, though perhaps the creation of new marine reserves might make even that possible. However, there is a feasible chance that sea urchins will recover in sufficient numbers to once again scrape away at the limestone reef in their billions, exposing enough surface space for corals to make a comeback. We must hope that this is the case.

The Interlocking Mosaic

A fundamental character of a coral reef system is the number of its closely interlocking parts. It is partly the interwoven nature of reef life that has led to its high diversity. Nothing can be more closely connected than a co-operative association between two different species, and it is commonly supposed that one reason for the success of corals themselves is their own interdependent relationship with algae. This close linkage, and the efficient nutrient recycling which became possible because of it, encourages coral growth in areas which are poor in nutrients, and this includes much of the ocean, especially far from land. This close association also extends to many other reef organisms: the shrimps and fish that share a burrow; the cleaner fish that remove parasites from much larger fish; the clown fish that live with impunity in the tentacles of large anemones and which lay their own eggs safely under their folds. Many examples exist and have been well illustrated.

Such is the resulting complexity of this ecosystem that scientists are still trying to understand it all. Questions such as: in what circumstances is a coral reef particularly fragile, and when is it robust and adaptable? There are good arguments on both sides, and it is a very important question today as we will see later. With so many species around, elimination of one or two might have very little consequence – another species might step into the missing role, and life on the reef might continue without too much disruption. This is the basis of the argument for reefs being robust, and it often seems to hold true. On the other hand, remove one or two other species, like the grazing sea urchins mentioned above, and apparent disorder and confusion occurs quite quickly, with the reef rapidly becoming a desolate algal plain. Or, introduce the disease called 'white-band disease'. In the Caribbean, this has caused the destruction of one species of shallow, wave-breaking coral almost entirely in the last two decades, causing major consequences and shoreline erosion.

Of course, both arguments are correct in different places and circumstances. It is a matter partly of which functional species is removed, of the degree to which it is removed, and also where it is removed from, in the sense that some species might be more important in one location than another. Another point is the well-debated question of 'scale'; something which is crucial on a small scale, say that of one reef or one bay or even one coral, may not

Steep reef slope with soft corals and schooling Anthia fish, Fiji, south Pacific. On steep surfaces and overhangs the light may be relatively dim, so many species of typical shallow-water corals cannot live there. Instead, the surface of the rock is generally covered with species of corals and soft corals which do not need light, as well as by molluscs, red algae and sponges which are also filter-feeding animals. The low light below an overhang can mimic the conditions on a much deeper part of the reef. Divers in these areas may see many forms of marine life not usually found within normal diving range. Here the animals feed mainly on zooplankton.

Sea fan growing out from a vertical reef wall, Papua New Guinea (left).

Basket star, a multi-armed relative of starfish, Flores Sea, Pacific (right).

be important on an ocean-wide scale, or vice versa. For example, we have seen that a certain amount of disturbance of the reef by grazers actually helps the biodiversity of the whole area by creating bare space for corals to settle, but obviously a massive disturbance could have the opposite effect. Trying to understand effects at different scales is one of the main areas of research today in complex systems like coral reefs.

Plankton

A major method of feeding by reef animals of all kinds is to capture plankton. Most reef animals produce huge numbers of eggs or larvae, not out of an altruistic desire to provide food for others, but in the desperate hope that some will survive. This is a good example of how evolution works. Larvae that make it might have had a slightly better genetic reason for surviving, so will pass on

that characteristic to their young. Plankton-feeding is found everywhere. Many species feed on plankton, some being ancient lineages of animals which today look quite outlandish, as do many fish and all corals. Crinoids and basket stars are relatives of the starfish, and are little more than collections of arms which are held up into the water to trap drifting prey. They are primitive, but have survived by trapping plankton for half-a-billion years, which is much longer than coral reefs, their present home, have been around. These are in addition to the almost continuous carpet of coral and soft coral polyps on the seabed with their stinging cells, and we have not even mentioned yet the swarms of planktonic feeding fishes.

Plankton has to avoid all these obstacles to survive, and over the millennia has developed two major strategies to help them do so. Firstly, many kinds have a daily rhythm: they live in crevices in the reef during the day, ascending higher in the water column at dusk, and descending again to hide at dawn. This is because they have to feed too, and need to get into the water column to capture their own food, which might consist of free-floating algae cells, and the times to do this, it seems, are dusk and dawn. The clouds of plankton in the water at these times can be striking. As with schooling fish, there is safety in numbers.

The premise of safety in numbers lies behind another mechanism that species have evolved to avoid having all their offspring devoured – synchronized spawning. In many parts of the world, spectacularly in the Great Barrier Reef, all corals spawn on the same night. On those nights, the sea appears filled with eggs, sperm bundles and larvae, and the strategy seems to be that of simply overwhelming the predators. Certainly predators congregate because they too have learned that this happens, and many billions of young are eaten, but when the appetite of the predators becomes sated, the surviving eggs or larvae will go free, for now at least. What is remarkable is that the synchronized spawning takes place across all the completely different species of corals, species which compete during the rest of the year, in a kind of inadvertent co-operation which benefits all.

These are just some examples of strategies for survival and of the interdependent relationship between different species on a reef. All species have developed their own tricks for survival, and those that do survive will be the ones with the most successful tricks, and will provide the genetic make up for the next generation. Several species change living habits as they age, several even change sex, and many change their habitats, depth or behavior. All species probably eventually become extinct, and many more species have once flourished and had their time in the sun than are here today. Any method a species uses to extend its chances will probably persist for a while longer, and the key point, perhaps, is the fact that what happens to one species is likely to affect many others too.

The Developing Crisis

Reefs have existed for 200 million years, since the Triassic. But in just the span of one human lifetime they have been assaulted by a series of blows which have reduced them to a state more precarious and fragile than any they have experienced before. About a third of the world's reefs have been killed or nearly so by misuse, overuse and abuse, and many reefs still classified as living are poor shadows of their former, vibrant selves. What caused this collapse? People, you may not be surprised to learn. But how, exactly? Too many people taking too much from them and inflicting several forms of pollution on them, all adding up to create a condition which the corals simply cannot withstand. Add to this the elimination of important species like herbivorous fishes, and we find that we have thoroughly disrupted the reefs' ecology.

Fishing

Firstly, there is overfishing, and several disastrous methods of doing so. In a number of countries, explosive blasting can be heard and seen, and felt by a diver in the water – a kind of dull hammer-blow. The blasts rupture fish swim bladders, which give fish their correct buoyancy. Following a blast, killed or injured fish are collected, though many are missed and rot. The results on the corals are obvious; in the length of time it takes to blink, the area turns from a colorful, vibrant and living reef to a flattened field of rubble, a bare plain instead of a three-dimensional structure, which an instant before provided shelter to thousands of different species.

Dynamite is a common explosive, usually acquired illegally by fishermen. Alternatively, they make explosives from various mixes of fertilizers stuffed into glass bottles. These practices are highly dangerous, as many people have lost their lives, but such is their desperation for protein or an income. The area lost with each blast is several square yards, and in some parts of the world blasts are incessant. Large reefs may be completely worked over in a month, and the rate of recovery, if the reef is allowed to recover at all before a repeat assault, is perhaps half a century. There are plans to monitor some reefs with hydrophones to detect this activity, but the will to stop it is generally missing, as the short-term rewards are great enough to persuade officials to turn a blind eye.

Another kind of destructive fishing is with cyanide. Squirted into crevices it captures especially desirable fish that are shipped thousands of miles to expensive restaurants. These fish generally recover (though the corals don't), and you may see them next in those little tanks in elegant restaurants where diners select one to eat. The diner probably does not know that a large patch of coral reef was poisoned to capture their meal.

But the sheer intensity of net fishing is now enough to cause a problem. Carnivorous and large herbivorous fish are pursued relentlessly, and their removal has turned many reefs into mounds of limestone covered with seaweed, as we have seen. Many once luxuriant Caribbean reefs are now domes of seaweed with just a few surviving scattered corals, a ghost of their former glory. There are too many people trying to take too much from the reef.

Construction and Industry

Direct coral mining has been a problem in several places. For example, in the Maldive island chain, in Sri Lanka and many parts of Southeast Asia, the easily excavated coral rock is a prime building material. Reefs in all oceans have been stripped of corals and blocks of limestone for building. This good, local rock is almost free, or at least freely available. You

Reef fishing is not always an idyllic occupation (above). Rising populations of millions of hungry people depend on reefs for their protein, and desperately try to catch more and more, both for food and a little spare cash. The corals of this reef in Indonesia appear to be in good condition, but an increasing shortage of fish could lead to the use of dynamite or poisons, such as cyanide (left).

A hawksbill turtle on the Great Barrier Reef, Australia. Sea turtles of all species are now protected because of past over-exploitation. The plates of the hawksbill shell were used to create ornamental buckles, combs, handbag clasps and similar non-essential trinkets, and the demand for hawksbill turtles created a slaughter of these attractive animals.

can turn it into lime if you heat it in kilns and use that for building too. In islands like the Maldives, protective reef flats have been lowered by about 2 feet (more than half a meter) because for years local people have waded out and prised millions of tons of corals from the shallows at low tide. Of course, this eventually removed the natural breakwater which stopped storm waves and, only recently, quite a lot of Malé, the capital city of the Maldives, was lost to a storm as a result.

Real estate is another problem. What property is nicer than a shorefront home, overlooking the sea? Put a lot of landfill on a reef, and build on that! Unfortunately, a lot of shallow reefs have been killed in this manner, most spectacularly in Middle Eastern countries. The resulting construction may well be striking but so, unfortunately, is the damage inflicted just below the water.

Another result of modern man's activities is the vast quantity of silt dumped into shallow seas. This may come directly from dredging, but mostly comes from poor farming methods in the inland watershed. Many badly farmed areas lose dozens of tons of topsoil from every acre (about 80 tons per hectare) every year. This ends up in the shallow sea as silt, blanketing reefs under choking sediment.

Industrial effluents can be a problem too, but generally are not as great as some would make out. It is easy to blame industrial polluters for all our ills — fishermen who overfish until there is nothing left to catch commonly blame pollution. Politicians who have long neglected any form of sensible and thoughtful coastal planning also blame pollution, as do many other groups. They may be right in certain local areas, but usually it's just about passing the buck. Massive funds are spent on controlling a bit of metal pollution here, and a bit of pesticide pollution there, but these problems are trivial compared with the main sources of disruption — the rise in nutrients and sediments that comes from sewage and poor land-use practices. These are, however, the most difficult to control. The resulting nutrients are a marvelous fertilizer for seaweed, and if we add to this the overfishing of herbivores which might have eaten that seaweed, then the results should not surprise us.

Diseases have also caused havoc. Some diseases affect corals directly – 'white-band disease', 'black-band disease' and others have marched through entire populations of corals in recent decades. Most striking in the Caribbean is that which killed off almost all the shallow-water Elkhorn coral, whose huge sturdy branches provided an essential wave break in shallow water. Those once glorious forests of tough corals are now piles of rubble, and shorelines and beaches are eroding in many places. In several places roads and buildings are undercut, and beaches near expensive hotels now have no sand at all, leaving jagged rock – not what you paid a small fortune to lie on during a vacation.

Global Warming

Recently another impact has hit coral reefs in a way which could dwarf all the others – the ocean surface is warming. In the 1980s and again in 1998, great shifts in sea and air temperatures caused massive climate changes. We heard about it often in its many guises: flooding in Central America, drought in many parts of Africa, scorching heat in many areas and unusual chills in others. The most famous part of this phenomenon is known as El Niño, the 'Christ Child', a South American event which starts near Christmas time and damages the fishing livelihood of so many people of that region. In much of the tropics, however, this climatic aberration led to a rise of water temperatures by just a degree or two, for a few weeks. Corals were killed in droves, especially in the Indian Ocean. The first effect was that they bleached – that is, they responded to the heat by expelling their symbiotic algae and so almost all of their color, showing the white limestone beneath. Then, they died. Bleaching has been recorded for a long time, and probably an observant diver will always have seen a coral or two on any dive suffering from this. They commonly recovered, but after the recent episode they almost all died. These events have happened before, but are increasing now in both their frequency and severity.

Black-band disease killing a brain coral (above). These are Caribbean species, a sea where many coral diseases have caused havoc in the past 20 to 30 years. The causes are commonly unknown, but have been related to pollution from agriculture and towns.

In many countries, corals are dug-up for use as building materials, usually using crowbars (right). This kills the corals and destroys the reefs, reducing their ability to act as breakwaters protecting islands.

In whole island groups, especially in the Indian Ocean, coral death was enormous. Many small patches usually escaped, presumably from fluke combinations of cool-water currents. Sometimes, deeper corals survived, as maybe some did in lagoonal passes where cooler water from deeper parts of the ocean flowed through, but mostly they didn't. It was a complicated pattern which is still being researched. Soft corals were killed off too. In 1998, the last year of El Niño, the Indian Monsoon failed, winds dropped, allowing the sea to become calm, and so more sunlight with its harmful ultraviolet rays penetrated shallow water and, combined with a rise in temperature, the effect was lethal. At the turn of the millennium, the view on perhaps most of the reefs of the Indian Ocean, and elsewhere, was one of bare rock. Corals were eroding, now gray instead of colored. Branching corals were often still upright, but dead, ghostly, and covered with a fine fur

French angelfish, off the Florida coast.

composed of small algae. A year or two later, these had mostly collapsed. Large expanses of table corals provided perhaps the most vivid, silent sentinels to the scale of the disaster. Many were still upright, but with fraying edges, or were recently toppled. In sites that had experienced a storm, maybe only their thicker, central stumps were left. Time and again, sites that used to have most of their surface covered by live corals and soft

One group of corals called porites *has survived global warming much better than most, Hawaii.*

63

corals now had only a scattering left. A vast natural treasure was lost from many places.

Is there hope? Well, yes and no. Partly it is a race between new growth and further decay. Some corals survived probably everywhere, and we know now that those survivors are reproducing again. It has been a relief to see large numbers of juveniles dotted all over, and if these grow up, then the problems would be solved, would they not? Well, perhaps. There are several crucial points. Firstly, erosion from waves and burrowing organisms is continuing fast, and the question we have to answer is: which will win, erosion or new growth? Research has begun in an attempt to answer this question, but we do not know yet which way that coin will fall. Secondly, this effect came on top of many other problems, such as pollution, the impacts of which continue. A third point is that sea surface temperatures are rising much faster than before in several places. One of the most affected places is the Indian Ocean with its huge expanses of coral reefs. Here, both sea and air temperatures have risen by about 1°C or even more in just 25 years – a large rise in an already warm ocean where many species were already living near the edges of their tolerance. Corals which survived are indeed breeding again, but if warming episodes repeat themselves, we cannot be sure what the next result will be. When we extend our graphs of temperature rise into the future we notice that in a very few years the temperature each year will reach the values which caused the mass destruction of the coral in 1998.

Several people have asked 'Is this not all part of a natural, basic rhythm, something that has happened regularly?' The answer is that the corals that died in droves during the closing decades of the second millennium included those which were hundreds of years old, so we know that this scale of event cannot have happened for that long at least. And cores drilled from Caribbean reefs have also shown that it probably has not happened for about 3000 years. The complex issues of human causes of destruction cannot be avoided for much longer, though many will try to do so. In any case, natural or man-induced, it does not really matter which it is, does it? We need now to guard against the consequences, whatever the causes.

Conclusion

I suspect that the reefs of the world will recover from the blows they are receiving, for they are resilient structures. But it will be a close-run thing, and we probably will not end up with such glorious biological constructions as we have known them to be. A lot of research is being conducted into causes of coral reef problems, into the details and the exact mechanisms to determine what are the weak links in this enormously complicated ecosystem. We must understand, too, the links that reefs have with other ecosystems, for all systems live or hang together to some degree. Interconnected ecosystems may be on adjacent coasts, though those may also be under threat. Or sometimes they may be connected over huge distances, for example by clouds of contaminated dust which can be seen on satellite images flowing to the Caribbean from North Africa. The ultimate widespread issue might be warming of the sea, the effects of El Niño, which is an issue of global proportions. Global issues are harder to tackle, but we must understand them or we may waste our efforts on futile measures.

We must also devise better methods whereby the daily needs of people who depend on reefs may be reasonably met without weakening the whole system, and we must determine what may be extracted without triggering a collapse. Many entire countries still have really no idea how much they can safely extract, and don't learn until their reef fishery collapses. One immediate prospect of allowing stocks of fish and their essential protein to recover lies in creating marine reserves in which large adults can spawn sufficiently to re-stock large areas around them. But local people have been suspicious of closed areas and of rules imposed from outside their community. Consequently, education, as well as research to determine where, and how big the protected area should be, are both

After the El Niño of 1997-8 corals bleached in many parts of the world when the sea water warmed. The finely branched corals (left) were particularly vulnerable, and died in their billions.

essential. Where both are done, the coastal people and the reef both become prime beneficiaries. Directed aid is also needed, with design input from those who understand reefs. This applies to all ecosystems; at present aid is determined too much at political levels for it ever to be very effective. All too often aid will target one facet of a problem without considering harmful 'downstream' effects which negate any initial benefits. For example, many well-meaning aid projects have developed flat coastal land, only to be surprised when the wider local ecosystem declines or dies. Ecosystems are integrated things, none more so than reefs, and in the end it is only the survival of a country's ecosystems which will enable the people that are supported by them to survive. People do not prosper when the environment around them fails, especially in societies where people are so immediately and obviously linked to natural resources as they are in tropical coastal communities.

There are just a couple of thousand coral reef scientists in the world, and the same number again whose research takes them to the fringes of this remarkable system every now and again – one for each 1000 miles (1600 kilometers) of reef. This is not very much for the ocean's richest and most diverse ecosystem. At conferences around the world, and in scientific articles in technical journals, problems and answers are researched and analyzed. Many of the problems and their solutions are in fact quite straightforward, scientifically at least. The solutions need to be implemented, of course. Those who live and depend on coral reefs include some of the world's poorest and most marginalized people, and they need us all to speak for them as best we can. It may be a romantic and beautiful environment, but that makes us forget it is a tough one too.

Reefs are, to most of us, far away places for exotic holidays, but they are also crucial habitats supporting millions of people living beside them at near-subsistence level. But there is hope, and that hope will come from understanding how reefs work, what problems afflict them, learning how to solve them, and by people persuading authorities that they matter to us all.

Distribution of the World's Coral Reefs

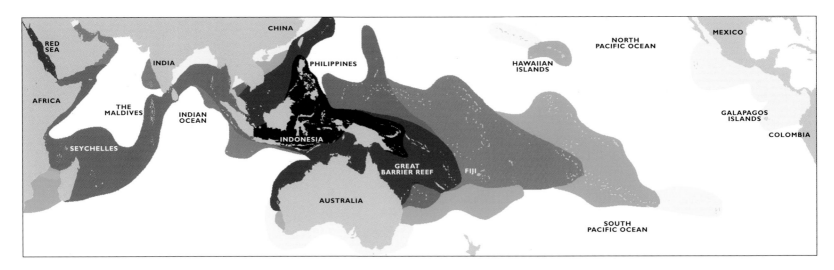

Coral reefs in the Indian and Pacific Oceans. Colored areas show the extent of coral reefs, and the color used shows the diversity (number of species) of reef-building corals in each zone. Highest diversity is around Indonesia and the Philippines. Across the Pacific, diversity declines from this high point, but extensive reefs occur right across to Polynesia and Hawaii. Reefs also occur off the Americas, but with fewer species. Across the Indian Ocean coral diversity remains high, and is especially high in the Red Sea. Reefs occur wherever there is suitable shallow continental shelf or islands, but die away in parts such as the northern Arabian Sea where conditions are unsuitable.

The colored sections on this map show the extent of coral reefs in the Atlantic. The Caribbean to southern Florida are the richest areas, with less rich sites in the Gulf of Mexico and Bermuda. Off Brazil, reefs occur with different sets of species. On the eastern side of the Atlantic there are widespread, scattered corals off Africa and its offshore island groups, but no good reefs.

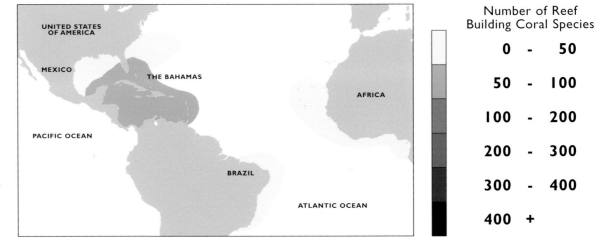

Number of Reef Building Coral Species

	0 - 50
	50 - 100
	100 - 200
	200 - 300
	300 - 400
	400 +

Coral and Coral Reef Facts

Two Main Groups of Corals

Corals that build reefs need light, because they contain algal cells, and so are limited to shallow water, but they grow fast. An equal or greater number of small species are found across the world, which are not 'reef-building', occurring mainly in deep, dark or cold water.

Growth Rates

The fastest branching corals may grow about 4 inches (10 centimeters) per year, so that a table coral with branches growing all-round may expand in diameter by 8 inches (20 centimeters) per year. Most grow much slower, about 0.08 to 0.4 inches (0.2 to 1 centimeters) per year for most boulder corals. They may grow in seasonal steps, and cores through them show annual growth rings, similar to trees.

Ages

From the evidence of growth rings, chemistry and radio isotopes, large boulder corals may be several hundred years old – 750 years seems to be the present known record, so these are probably the world's oldest animals.

Breeding

Some are male or female, but most are hermaphrodites. A number broadcast both eggs and sperm into the water where they fertilise, others release sperm which fertilise eggs inside other coral polyps where they are then brooded. New planulae develop, which can swim a little and are moved considerable distances by currents before settling to grow into another colony. Most species reproduce by fragmenting in many kinds of unusual ways too.

Other Reef Animals

There are approximately as many soft corals as corals, and most of those seen on reefs contain algae. There are over 5000 species of reef fish, and a similar number of molluscs (excluding tiny species which are commonly overlooked). About 2000 species of the starfish group include many conspicuous species too. There are great numbers of several groups of worms, hundreds of sponges, and thousands of species of what are commonly called 'lesser groups', all making up one of the richest ecosystems on the planet.

Kinds of Reefs

Three major classes of reef are recognised: atolls, barrier reefs and fringing reefs. But all intergrade, depending on their age and whether the ground they sit on is rising, sinking or is temporarily stable, and many kinds like patch reefs are simply small versions of almost any of these. There is only a poor relationship between numbers of corals on a reef and the size or strength of the reef; some high diversity reefs are small and inconspicuous, while some of the huge oceanic atolls subjected to the strongest wave energy may have only a small number of coral species.

Growth of Reefs

Reefs grow much more slowly than the corals on them, partly because the corals are immediately eroded and turned to sand when they die. Sand production on reefs may be several pounds per year for every square yard. Large quantities are lost to deeper water, but much gets piled onto shores where they form the brilliant white sand so characteristic of coral islands.

Index

Entries in bold indicate pictures

Recommended Reading

Popular Titles

Amin, M., Willetts, D., & Skerrett, A., *Aldabra, World Heritage Site*, Camerapix Publishers, 1995.

Aw, M., *Metamorphosea. A 24 Hour Sojourn on the Great Barrier Reef*, Ocean Geographic, 1995.

Humann, P., *Reef Coral Identification*, 3 volumes, New World Publications Inc., 1993.

Veron, J.E.N., *Corals of the World*, 3 volumes, AIMS and CRR, 2000.

Scientific Titles

Birkland, C., *Life and Death of Coral Reefs*, Chapman and Hall, 1997.

Karlson, R.H., *Dynamics of Coral Communities*, Klurver, 1999.

McClanahan, T., Sheppard, C.R.C., Obura, D., *Coral Reefs of the Indian Ocean*, Oxford University Press, 2000.

Spalding, M.D., Ravilious, C., & Green, E.P., *World Atlas of Coral Reefs*, University of California Press, 2001.

Veron, J.E.N., *Corals in Space and Time*, Comstock and Cornell, 1995.

Biographical Note

Dr Charles Sheppard has participated in more than 1000 research dives on coral reefs around the world, including the Caribbean, Red Sea, Indian Ocean and the Great Barrier Reef. Based on his experiences he has written over 100 articles and ten books on marine science and on the natural history and the future of reefs. A lecturer at the University of Warwick, England, he also spends time teaching and researching in developing countries on behalf of aid and development organizations. He lives in England with his family.